The Emma Press Anthology of

MILDLY EROTIC VERSE

The Emma Press Anthology of
MILDLY EROTIC VERSE

edited by Rachel Piercey and Emma Wright

Julia Bird ○ Mel Denham ○ Joy Donnell
Hugh Dunkerley ○ Kirsten Irving ○ Amy Key
Anja Konig ○ Ikhda Ayuning Maharsi
Julie Mullen ○ Richard O'Brien ○ Emma Reay
Kristen Roberts ○ Jacqueline Saphra
Lawrence Schimel ○ Stephen Sexton ○ Jon Stone
Sara-Mae Tuson ○ Ruth Wiggins ○ Jerrold Yam

THE EMMA PRESS

THE EMMA PRESS

First published in Great Britain in 2013
by The Emma Press Ltd

Poems copyright © individual copyright holders 2013
Selection copyright © Rachel Piercey and Emma Wright 2013
Illustrations and introduction copyright © Emma Wright 2013

All rights reserved.

The right of Rachel Piercey and Emma Wright to be identified
as the editors of this work has been asserted by them in accordance
with the Copyright, Designs and Patents Act 1988.

ISBN 978-0-9574596-2-5

A CIP catalogue record of this book
is available from the British Library.

Printed and bound in Great Britain.

theemmapress.com

Contents

Introduction   ix

TIGHT DRESS —— Amy Key —— 1
HARE —— Hugh Dunkerley —— 2
PINKIE MINIMUS —— Ikhda Ayuning Maharsi —— 5
TRICKSTER —— Joy Donnell —— 6
BIRCH —— Ruth Wiggins —— 7
RADIOCARBON DATING —— Anja Konig —— 9
HAVE YOU IMAGINED HAVING SEX WITH ME? —— Emma Reay —— 10
THE JACKAL AND THE MOON —— Sara-Mae Tuson —— 12
THE STUDENT —— Kirsten Irving —— 16
PRIZE —— Jerrold Yam —— 17
TO SEPTEMBER, FROM JUNE —— Mel Denham —— 18
WEAPONRY —— Jon Stone —— 20
CARAMEL SWIRL —— Amy Key —— 21
BEYOND THE CARROT —— Julie Mullen —— 22
PRESS PLAY —— Julia Bird —— 24
THE FROZEN MAN —— Jacqueline Saphra —— 27
GLAMOUR —— Jon Stone —— 28
FAIRY TALE —— Lawrence Schimel —— 29
THE MISSING —— Joy Donnell —— 31
MAGICIAN'S ASSISTANT —— Richard O'Brien —— 32
A COLLECTION OF TINY ISLANDS —— Sara-Mae Tuson —— 34
COOL CHANGE BEFORE MIDNIGHT —— Kristen Roberts —— 35
SECOND CIRCLE —— Stephen Sexton —— 36

Acknowledgments   39

About the poets   41

Introduction

I was pretty excited when erotic literature hit the bestseller charts in 2011. It felt like another aspect of human sexuality had entered the mainstream, as thousands of people ruled that there was nothing shameful about wanting to read about sex and different sexual practices, even in public.

But it annoyed me that many of these bestsellers weren't terribly erotic. They contained lashings of sex and were enjoyable romances, but they didn't strike me as genuinely sexy and thrilling, and I wondered if their success was contributing to the misinterpretation of 'eroticism' as equivalent with 'sex'. This distinction between 'Popular Erotica' and 'Genuinely Erotic Fiction' might seem snobby or a matter of personal opinion, but when a society's attitude towards sex is still a work in progress it feels important to assert the individual identity of eroticism and understand it as a much broader, looser concept than sex, for all that they have in common.

My instinct is that eroticism exists around the edges of sex, in the anticipation and desire and in memories and associations. It exists on both cerebral and carnal levels, and it's hard to define because each person's sense of it is utterly unique. It can be wild, hilarious, beautiful and alarming; difficult to describe but the easiest thing to spot once you know what you're looking for – maybe a tiny leap in the stomach or a burst of exclamation marks in the brain.

I wanted to create a book which celebrated the diversity and eccentricity of eroticism and human sexuality, in relation to the physical mechanics of sex as well as apart from it. Poetry is the ideal medium for examining and communicating elusive concepts without flattening them, and so *The Emma Press Anthology of Mildly Erotic Verse* was born.

I worried that some aspects of the brief ('mildly', 'erotic', 'verse') might deter some people, but my co-editor Rachel Piercey and I ended up collecting over 170 submissions from all over the world. The standard of submissions was high, and there were several which we liked a lot but had to let go because they didn't fit with our vision for the book. Some were more romantic than erotic; some were sexual and nothing more. There was a whole tranche of darkly erotic poems which piqued our interest but made us realise that we wanted the book to be enjoyable and encouraging, not depressing.

Which isn't to say that there are no discomfiting poems in our final selection. Quite the contrary: we wanted the anthology to skate the line between teasingly sketchy and uncomfortably raw, and I hope there are poems in this book which will surprise readers and challenge their notions of what other people – and they – find erotic. Some, like Julia Bird's *Press Play* and Kristen Roberts' *Cool change before midnight*, approach their subject from a distance, positively vibrating with restraint, while others, like Anja Konig's *Radiocarbon Dating* and Emma Reay's *Have you imagined having sex with me?* are exhilaratingly direct.

Rawness is a key part of this collection's identity, and we were conscious when selecting the poems that we wanted the book as a whole to deliver an unglossed depiction of eroticism. We wanted it to be true to the reality of adult life, which is full of mess and complications; there is space for romance and tenderness, and even the odd fairytale, but in real life erotic moments occur between the mundane and the distinctly unerotic, and are no less erotic for that. *Tight Dress*, by Amy Key, and Jon Stone's *Glamour* both examine human interactions on such an intimate level that our initial discomfort turns to awe. *Magician's Assistant*, by Richard O'Brien, takes place in a retail park and a budget hotel room; Julie Mullen's *Beyond the Carrot* kicks off after a hard day at work; and the speaker in *To September, from June*, by Mel Denham, smells of car-exhaust while her lover dreams of caravans.

A more ambitious aim for the anthology, which goes back to my irritation with the bestselling erotic novels, was to find a new vocabulary for eroticism and sex. I feel we have reached a point

INTRODUCTION

where the standard phrases for evoking eroticism have lost their ability to surprise and inspire, and every stock verb, noun, adjective and adverb makes sex sound cartoonish and unappealing. Some words just need to be used more sensitively, while others should probably be laid to rest. A penis has never sounded good when throbbing, never mind the fact of being called a penis. The poets we found understood this, and among my favourite words in this anthology are new words such as *resolving, smashed, bones, spoon, elasticity, moulding, inhaled, trace, shallowing*; and more familiar ones like *warm, suck, swollen, stroke, wet*.

I have high hopes for this little book, which is the product of so many talented poetic imaginations. It has been a privilege working with Rachel: editing a mildly erotic anthology with a close friend is every bit as fun as you might expect, but editing a poetry anthology with a gifted poet in her own right is illuminating and awe-inspiring in equal measure. It has also been a pleasure working with all the poets who rose to the challenge and helped make my vision a reality. I could not be more delighted with the poems assembled inside these covers, and I feel tremendously lucky to have encountered such witty, generous, insightful writers. Eroticism is alive and well in their hands.

Emma Wright
July 2013
Winnersh

*The Emma Press Anthology
of Mildly Erotic Verse*

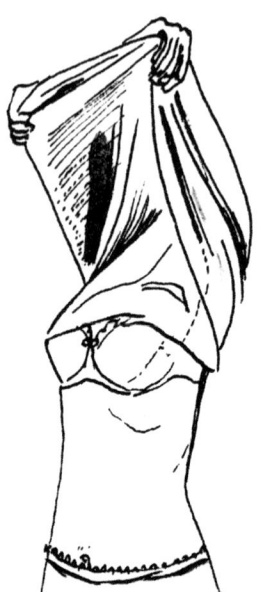

Tight Dress

I'm in the tight dress. The one that prevents dignified sitting.
The tight dress suggests I'm prepared to be undressed.
Do my thighs flash through the seams?
I try to remember if the bed is made, or unmade.
The wind is wrapping up the sound of our kissing.
I wonder should I undress first or should you undress first.
I'm not sure I can take off the dress in a way that looks good.
I consider if I should save up sex until morning.
We are far gone and I'm better at kissing when sober.
I find that your earlobes provide the current fascination.
On my bedside table are three glasses of water and my favourite love letter.
I try to untie your shoes in a way that is appalling.

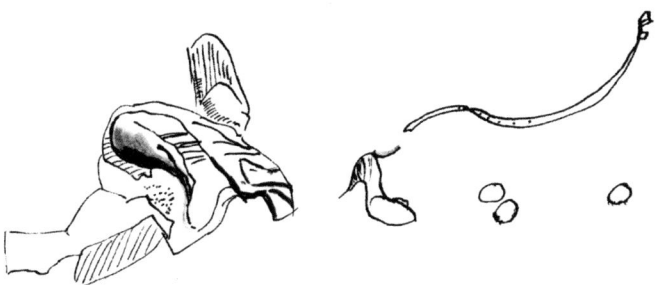

Hare

for Bethan

*

Snakes that cast your coats for new,
Chameleons that alter hue,
Hares that yearly sexes change.
>   Fletcher: *The Faithful Shepherdess*

I

You were surprised by its huge ears,
alert and stiff in the long grass

its masculine nose,
the lithe terrier-like body.

We were almost on it
when the hare erupted into flight

something more like a deer
than a rabbit in the way it ran

bounding in fast surefooted leaps
across the astonished field

until it veered suddenly, rose into the air
and was gone in the dusk of the wood

leaving only this impression
warm in the still unravelling grass.

II

Warm in the still unravelling sheets,
I run my fingers down your spine

trace the soft vestigial hair of an animal
that only minutes ago I held

bucking in my arms, a fierceness
I'd never imagined, straining for release

a changeling that slipped between my fingers
and was gone with a cry

now resolving itself back into you.

Pinkie Minimus

I asked you to keep the promise
using your, my Pinkie Minimus,
like when we were children.

I hoped that you would keep your promise
that we made by Pinkie Minimus
like when we were moppets.

But what did you do
but suck my Pinkie Minimus,
wrestled with worms and germs.

Yes o yes o
my Pinkie Minimus
has been sucked,
licked by your blunt tongue.
O no o no no
what I asked was the promise
of lost childhood,
two Pinkie Minimus
linked to each other.

Yes o yes o
we should have put our wedding rings
on the tiny
platoon
Pinkie Minimus.

Trickster

Wolves either come or they don't come.
She swears every rabbit or fox or crane
could fall prey by dawn
and where would that leave the laws of the universe?

Under such stars
my legs are open and chancy.
This intimacy is at best
peregrine
so I confess to not know myself any more or less,

regardless,

I suspect our breasts will become the storytellers;
somehow
all my damages get tricked into touch.
If between her thighs rests a border town too often
mysterious,
it tastes swollen and will surely riot, tonight.

Birch

Prostrate birch –
what's with all the reaching?

So keen for something
that you can't get straight.

You lean. Invite me to
saddle up. Strong-backed

you speak to me
in mushroom and lichen.

Go on,
green my tongue.

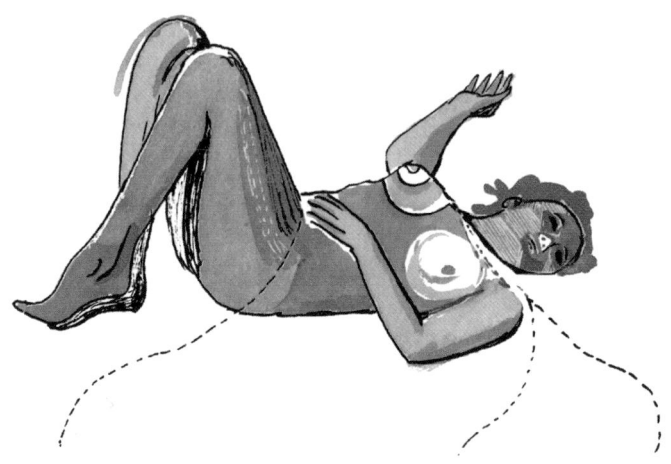

Radiocarbon Dating

It's no longer done –
comparing a woman's body to a landscape –
buttock hillocks, dales and deltas –

politically incorrect. But I want you
in charge of manning up an expedition to undefined
white spaces on my map. I want you

to use your scientific training, evaluate
my forestation, measure the circumference of both
polar caps. You can examine drilling cores

to reconstruct my seismic history. The positions
of tectonic faults, degree of liquefaction
of the crust and mantle imply

tremors are possible and could be more
than model settlements can handle.

You can still shift your paradigm, embrace
a post-colonial sentiment and keep your footprint light.

Have you imagined having sex with me?

Have you imagined having sex with me?
Planned exactly how it would be?
Have you pictured all the faces?
The sighs, the eyes, the grimaces?
Have you schemed how we'd get started?
Am I flash-naked, legs parted?
Or maybe there's some back-story,
Of brave knights and morning glory?
Or a plumber, a pizza boy.
And what am I – coquette or coy?
Am I Russian? Or am I Thai?
With skin on thin or fat on thigh?
Am I a pliable, edible fool?
Or cougar-clawed, matured and cruel?

Do I like you? Do you hope I do?
Do you wish I were more open with you?
I might be Flora, or Fauna, or Eve, or Dawn,
Alder Trees, Laurel Leaves, Spider, Swan;
I am 5 ft. 7, fair, Caucasian;
Territory vulnerable to invasion;
I am all states; I am armies campaigning;
I am trying and taxing and waxing and waning;
I'm in orbit; I'm a film on repeat;
I'm Victory, I'm cold, I'm young, I'm defeat.
I stretch for miles, and if you tried
To run, like a stream down a mountain's side,
More faithful than you meant to be,
You could run for hours and never leave me.

the jackal and the moon

give me your hand, he says,
jonquil eyes suspended by drink;
tightrope quick, he lurches towards
the doom of her red lips.

she smiles, unfurling her tiny paw,
with an arch look asks:
will you read it?
smacking her lips suggestively
like a jackal inhaling the steam
from the entrails of a kill
on a cold night.

I see a hand, he intones,
beginning the assault
with a flick of his tongue
in the centre of her palm.
a soft hand ...

softer than other hands?
she is very dangerous in this light,
the cool, white sheen of her cheeks glowing.
no better, he says. *no worse.*
and your eyes ...

no better? she waits,
breath bated.
your left eye being somewhat higher, perhaps ...
he considers, head tipped with whimsy.

her eyebrows bristle,
flecks of gold ignite in her eyes.

your neck ...
she clasps it protectively,
the five jewels of her fingertips
flexing possessively.
... as much like a neck as I have ever seen.

she hardens her heart, snaps
who do you think you are?
her white teeth cracking together,

a movie clapboard
proclaiming: *The End*!
she begins to turn away, hungry for other meat.

oh, but Biatista, he squeezes her palm.

I could make you howl
against the blood-soaked moon,
till the juices of our bodies overran ourselves.
if you smashed yourself against me,
I'd strip you like a taxidermist
strips a dead animal,

till the you you were was a husk
and the you you are is coated in musk,
thick as peanut butter,
straight from the jar ...

what's the matter with you?
don't you know how to talk to a lady?
her arch twang inhabits curiosity like an old fur coat,
as she purrs along his neckline, watching his pulse.

he thinks of how he'd like to bite
the virgin flesh of her clavicle,

sink his teeth into soft skin,
worrying at her woman's bones.

oh Biatista, you know I never lie,
your eye is an eye.
your hair, like hair anywhere.
but come with me
and we'll be good together,
that I guarantee.

Biatista gave a smile
which cut through his ribs
like a prison shiv,
curled up her claws and ...
came to him.

and the night was a night,
and the moon was a moon as bright
as the moon is wont to be,
and that's alright,
that's just as it should be.

The Student

It's 7am in the park. You're pretending
you don't see the grime-chested kendo student
drilling, *hakama* stretched into a theatre,
bokken now passing like a wing before him.
His forearms and fingers are lean, and you're feeling
his weight on your own and his hands on your wrists.
He brings down the sword with a shift of his hips.
Advances, quite cat-like, fresh sweat on a forelock.
Tonight you'll draw ronin in *hicho* like herons.
Tonight you'll be dreaming of jostling red fish.

Prize

Like a swig of medicine, the undressing is easy;
I watch the sun rehearse over the arena,
its lonely eye laying mahogany sheets
on a row of strangers. Then, when it rages
enough for a change, I slip
soundlessly in the pool, legs
pivoting for the kick-off, as if recalling the force with
which a man enters my quiet chamber. And the sun
agrees, setting live wires over a turquoise floor;
I am drawn to its audacity, its electrical charm
tamed by water. Later in the changing
room we would smile, just short of crime, desperation
stiffening like a drug as we become
conjoined, at the pelvis, every breath
also traced with time's impatient handwriting.
It ends as it may only end, wrenched
free to false safety, as if afraid
of intimacy. I press a finger
to the slag, to my lips,
its awkward musk
stinging like genius. By then
you would have gone, so sure of
diving into another life.

To September, from June

I am already mythologising.
Maybe that's why I invoke a Greek hero's quest
as we descend the steep stairs
to a Smith Street streaked with late-night rain

In your version of heaven you live in a caravan by the sea
in mine there's a city apartment
a decorous distance from your
untrustworthy hands

We would meet
but not too often
having had plenty of practice caressing
the palpable texture of absence

In my dim-lit room cluttered
with books I would taste
salt on your lips

On your sheets we'd dishevelled
within earshot of the moan and sigh
of waves you'd bury
your face in my hair's faint
car-exhaust scent

Don't let me get too old you say as if
I can stop time like you
kill speech when you put your mouth to mine – *Oh
loosen the tongues of my mute body*

In place of that paradise on which the sun may never rise
know this instead:
tonight when your familiar voice
speaks and your familiar hand
moves

It's a present
pleasure I can't grasp to keep
my own hand
table-bound and calm
the clamour from my – *take me* – traitorous heart.

Weaponry

When Adrienne goes through the metal detector,
it lets out a cry to the nearby attendant,
who outlines her shape with his prominent baton.

Cases heap up at the end of the belt
like dead in a pit, and the x-ray of Adrienne's
things is a catch from the luminous deep:

anglerfish, viperfish, barbeled dragonfish.
Bodies re-armour themselves with possessions
– meat of the wallet and chainmail of keys –

and Adrienne's clothes move the baton to humming
what might be the start of a conjugal hymn
at her thigh and her breast and her other thigh too.

Slowly she sheds every one of her talismans
(pencils, a hair clip, a dozen spent tickets)
until she's as light as her bones and her bones.

Caramel Swirl

Mine is the caramel with salt, a skirt and a tinselled belly.
It swirls like my swishy hem. Makes me maudlin
like sea frets, like sweetness – a buttery throat.

I need something to do with my hands.

Take me and my caramels and swoon
with sweetheart films where the beauty eats
bon-bons from a satin box.

There is nothing worse than pouring my own bath.

I need something to do – caramel-glaze the silver,
spoon praline from a crystal bowl. Ruin myself.
There is nothing worse than darning my own slippers.

I need something to get my teeth into.

Beyond the Carrot

Harry was a veggie.
Harry was my nice neighbour in his
    elasticated cardigan;
        tattyhatted, fatted cravatted.
He was a theatrical agent,
drinking red wine and slinging the bottles into his
    ecologically sound
        black bin.
He had style but somehow
just too old-fashioned
for old-fashioned me.
I kept away.
I didn't like vegetarians.

Then one day just after a
battle of a day that made me weep on the train,
I slipped past his bin and I saw him naked, coming out of the bath.
He was standing there in the moonlight,
all damp and vegetarian,
and in the background I smelt carrots on the cook.

So I slammed my door.
Slammed it
for the hell of it
    and for his carrots
        and his tattyhattedness
            and my loneliness
and my longing for what lay beyond
the carrot.

I went in and changed.
I changed, and I changed again.
Then I bathed and I threw in cabbages, broccoli, aubergine,

I bathed in these vegetables,
caressed them, loved them, joined them.
The water was hot and steamy and I felt
    the earth
        I felt the soil
           I felt Harry's hat
              I felt
I felt crazy but I loved it
I felt awkward but I shunned it
I felt I was feeling for the first time.

I'd heard he bathed in vegetables
but I hadn't believed it till today,
when I smelt the carrot.

So I went to his bed.
I got out of the bath and I dripped wet over to number 8
and I went to Harry's bed
and there I saw a head
of cauliflower that made me feel
like an elasticity of coming;
an age, a time, a right time.
We caressed the head together,
then a cabbage,
and before I knew it Harry had plunged me into heaven,
Vegetarian Heaven!
Why had I waited so long to go veggie?

Press Play

I

Load too much credit in the jukebox
    and every single ever written
        starts to play at once.

Vocals and bass lines,
    choruses and middle eights,
        session brass, children's choirs, sitars

swept up in a high tide of soundwaves
    lining up and clicking home
        and wiping themselves out.

The composite hit
    is a white wall of sound.
        Decibels unreadable as silence.

II

Replay and overlay us the last time
    with every time that's gone before.
        You, me, and. You, me, or.

Touch is papered over touch
    like a ricked joint rubbed numb,
        or gooseflesh on sunburn.

Like a stack of transparencies
    held to the light, such
        chaotic couplings –

a pinned or stretching limb
    in every second of a circle, some
        bomb blast or star burst. Some chrysanthemum.

III

With the white noise on repeat,
    attune yourself till every cell
        buzzes like a snare drum

and pick them out:
    that run of double claps,
        Minnie's head-notes, shattering.

A low sliding scale of Tom,
    and the song that holds its nerve
        on the fadeout rainstorm.

The Frozen Man

At the cusp of the year in absolute dark
        she calls his name. She catches
                scatters of him in the soft cup of her hands
                      until he is too much to hold. He falls
                              and falls, until he covers the bed.

Slowly, she breathes him into warmth,
        her pink tongue patient against
                his white-blue beauty,
                      her body moulding him,
                            her legs embracing him.

She knows his coldness will not keep;
                before the spring, he will melt
                          complete from her hands.

Glamour

Beneath the boiled wool, he's just a skellybones,
and underneath the skellybones, a fumbling boy,
and underneath the boy, he's one of Jakey's twins,
and under that he's nothing but a bumblebee.
Peel back the bee and he's a coddled emperor,
and under that, she stumbles on a beery goon
but under that, none other than Hercule Poirot,
and underneath Poirot, he's just a boy again.

And she's a sweet thing underneath the stars and spurs,
a cloud beneath the sweet thing, and then under that
he finds a girl who sports a look of faint surprise,
but she too falls away and leaves a cinder smut.
The cinder smut's a cover; she's a grizzly bear
and then a toymaker and then a tomahawk,
and finally a girl who's been to Zanzibar,
a girl who thinks she might be an insomniac.

They know the thing to do tonight is sleekly slide
against each other's planes the way they do in films,
be spoon and syrup, glass and shadow, blade and blade.
But now the smell of overripeness overwhelms
the both of them, and out they slip from underneath
the glamours that had all but pinned them in their place,
two grubbied-up potato dolls with sticky breath
and all the more delighted for their ugliness.

Fairy Tale

Lying naked atop the sheets in the summer heat
his lumpy genitals press against his crotch
like a frog crouched
in the thick reeds of dark pubic hair.

'Kiss me,' they whisper,
'and I shall grow into a prince.'

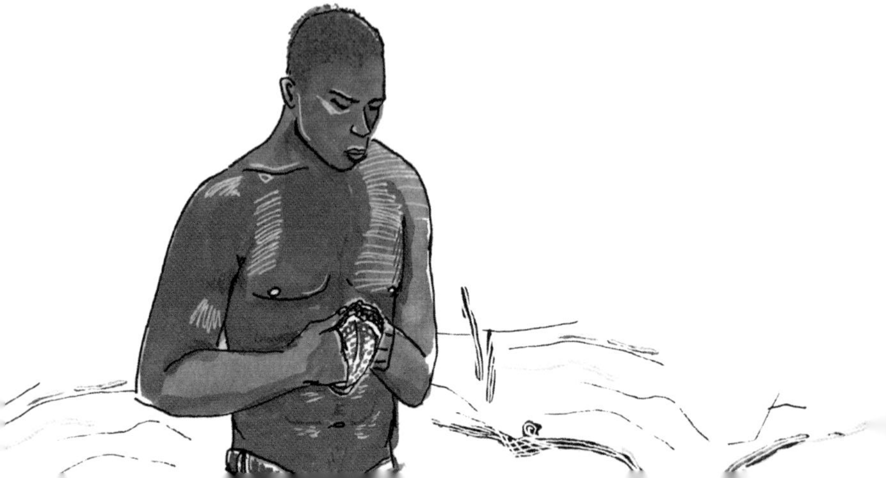

The Missing

Weeks later
she was resigned she'd lost her red silk thong forever.
While answering work emails, she imagined the airy crimson
victimized by crazy fates; [1] an unrealized bookmark
between pages
of *Cancer,*
dusty
below an abandoned bed
[2] flapping along the flagpole of devout Communists
[3] deconstruction at the mouths of feral dogs, in an alley,
ruined;
but the montage gave way to a hope he still had it,
its entirety enveloping his long fingers
and maybe while contemplating
its biography and the origin of the world
he closes his eyes.
Inhales.

Magician's Assistant

Legs. Released by the entrance song
they spread like an accordion,
collapse. I have been working on

resistance to your charms –
and failing that, my upper arms.
Dry ice evades all smoke alarms.

*

After the show I hold your cloak
above the dust of the retail park.
Step lightly, darling, through the dark.

Your sequined foot unsticks the clutch;
unchoreographed, our belts click shut.
An escapologist is never stuck.

One room. You clatter through the minibar;
your wrists, their first-time fire-thrower scars.
My heart's a sleeve that won't stop spilling scarves.

*

I'm breathless at your sleight of hand;
be good to me, the Great, the Grand.
The cushions levitate. I never see them land.

We climb inside in your velvet trunk,
dodge hidden drawers, gewgaws and junk,
half-dressed and more than halfway drunk,

and bring the lid down, plush with galaxies
that stroke your spine, lending their light to me.
I'm finding glitter in your hair for weeks.

*

Another town. You spin the box
then come toward me, blade aloft,
brushing my fingers when you turn the locks.

I curl my knees up, count to ten
and let you split me, put me back again.
Exhale. I was a different person then.

a collection of tiny islands

the memory of him is like a brick
through the window of her plans:
her wedding, a slow-moving iceberg,
has now breached the hull.

frozen in her white dress,
she remembers his long limbs,
the taste of his youth on her tongue.
she wanted to eat him, take him into herself.

the time they luxuriated in ...
dropping long and deep into hours –
she would be ashamed, now,
to hold someone's face
until she learnt the language of eyelashes,
the topographical importance of moles –
the archipelago in the sweet muscular curve
of his lower back.

and yet they were mostly inarticulate,
their talk breathless as she inhaled him.

she'd lick her fingertips,
trace her thoughts from pectoral to crown –
she wrote them down;
each wet, bare inch anointed
with the whorls and loops of love.

all this she longs to bottle up
and throw into the ocean,
someone else's problem,

so the boy's body becomes
the uncharted territory behind her eyes,
a collection of tiny islands.

Cool change before midnight

At ten we open the windows
and the cool air rolls in like a tide,
soothes the heat-sullen rooms
and settles the kids
in their sheet-tangled thrashing.

We shower in darkness
as though light itself holds warmth,
the water dancing on our skin
as the sour graffiti of the day streams away
and the relief of night unfurls.

Naked we run through the house,
flick our hair at each other
and feel the startling kiss of droplets
on flesh that's too seldom bare,
and trace their sliding trails with our tongues
under the pale eye of the moon.

Second Circle

We were alone, and we suspected nothing.
>   Dante Alighieri
>   (trans. Mandelbaum)

You've been going through each book and CD.
I've found the long black threads of your hair
in *Crash*, which you aren't ashamed to read aloud.

So with the wind as it is, yes, there
is a case for staying the night; branches
twist and slap at the picture window – where

I'll draw the blind – submitting evidence.
The streetlights have remade
the pressing oak trees into silhouettes.

All this in the wind makes a house of my bed.
The wind insists. The wind
is your breath shallowing on the back of my head.

I wake in the night with you behind
me and the wind slight at the window sill.
One twig
            scratching an inch of glass reminds me

you are not asleep
                    your hands are far from still.

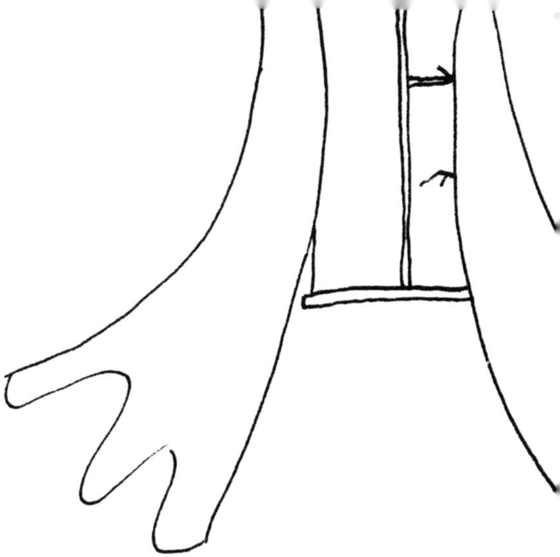

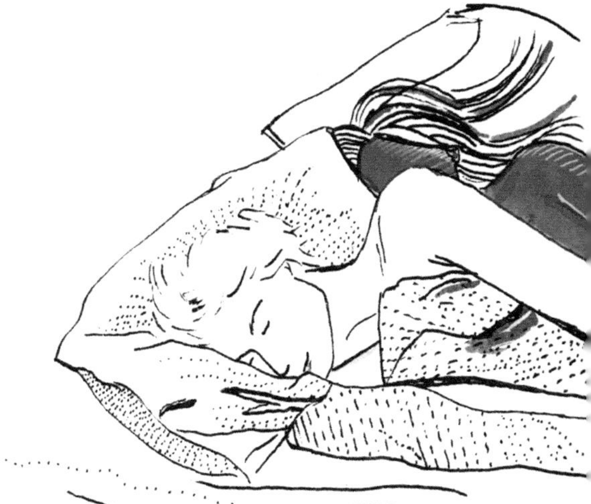

Acknowledgments

Acknowledgments and thanks are due to the original editors and publishers of some of the poems in this anthology:

Tight Dress, by Amy Key, first published in her debut pamphlet, *Instead of Stars* (tall-lighthouse, 2009).

Hare, by Hugh Dunkerley, first published in *Irish Pages*, Vol 4, Number 1, as well as appearing in Hugh's collection *Hare* (Cinnamon Press, 2010).

An earlier version of *The Jackal and the Moon*, by Sara-Mae Tuson, was published in *Loose Muse: An Anthology of New Writing by Women* (2012).

An earlier version of *Prize*, by Jerrold Yam, was first published in *Scattered Vertebrae* (Math Paper Press, 2013).

An earlier version of *Beyond the Carrot*, by Julie Mullen, first appeared in *Erotic Poetry for Vegans and Vegetarians* (2009).

Fairy Tale, by Lawrence Schimel, first appeared in *Deleted Names* (A Midsummer Night's Press, 2013).

The Missing, by Joy Donnell, first appeared in *Velvet Avalanche* (Satjah Projects, 2006).

About the poets

Julia Bird grew up in Gloucestershire and now lives in London. She works part-time for the Poetry School, and produces touring live literature shows as a freelancer. Her first collection *Hannah and the Monk* was published by Salt in 2008, and her second, *Twenty-Four Seven Blossom*, is due out in Autumn 2013.

Mel Denham lives in the literature-loving city of Melbourne. She's had a lifelong love affair with poetry, but has only recently begun writing it. She is working on a collection of poems about her other love, the postal system. Brief musings on this and other ephemera can be found at meldenham.com.

Joy Donnell is a writer, producer and former publicist living in Los Angeles by way of Georgia. Her work is published or forthcoming in anthologies printed by Beacon Press, Random House, St. Martin's Press and Alyson Books. She can be found online at www.twitter.com/doitinpublic.

Hugh Dunkerley grew up in Edinburgh and Bath and now lives in mildly erotic Brighton with his wife and young son. He has published one full collection, *Hare* (Cinnamon Press, 2010), in which sex and nature feature prominently. He is currently working on a new collection about fatherhood.

Kirsten Irving co-runs Sidekick Books with Jon Stone and her own poetry has been published by Happenstance and Salt. She normally writes a lot about robots. And schoolgirls too. And sometimes cannibals. Sexy robot schoolgirl cannibals.

Amy Key was born in Dover and grew up in Kent and the North East. She now lives and works in London. She co-edits the online journal *Poems in Which*. Her pamphlet *Instead of Stars* was published by tall-lighthouse in 2009. Her debut collection *Luxe* will be published by Salt in November 2013.

Anja Konig was raised in the German language and now writes in English. Her work has appeared in magazines in the UK and the US, including *Poetry Review*, *Poetry London*, *Smiths Knoll*, *Magma*, *The Stand*, *Cimarron Review*, and *The Washington Square Review*.

Ikhda Ayuning Maharsi has worked in television, advertising and as a scriptwriter on a sitcom in Indonesia. She performed her poetry for the first time in 2011, at Cité Internationale Universitaire de Paris. She now lives in Naples, where she is enjoying her new role as mother to her little boy Corentin.

Julie Mullen is a Liverpool performance poet. She has performed at The Assembly Rooms Edinburgh, The Chelsea Arts Club, Soho House, and The Groucho Club. Brian Patten commented on her book *Erotic Poetry For Vegans & Vegetarians*, 'Does for sprouts what Wordsworth did for daffodils.' She can be found on www.thewordcafe.co.uk.

Richard O'Brien's first pamphlet, *your own devices*, appeared in 2009 on tall-lighthouse press. His work has featured in *Poetry London*, the *Erotic Review*, and *The Salt Book of Younger Poets*. His blog, *The Scallop-Shell* (thescallopshell.wordpress.com), is dedicated to the close reading of contemporary poetry.

After graduating from Oxford in 2012, **Emma Reay** was a little lost. She tried a few different things but soon decided to give adult life the slip and hitchhike around America, where she may still be right now. She has a keen interest in photography and her travel blog can be found at www.thenorthship.co.uk.

Kristen Roberts is an Australian poet and full time mum. Her poetry has won the Michael Thwaites and *page seventeen* poetry competitions and has been published in Australian journals, which sometimes feels unbelievable when considered from the midst of Wiggles sing-alongs and toilet training. Kristen is currently polishing her first manuscript.

Jacqueline Saphra has won several awards including first prize in the Ledbury Poetry Competition. Her pamphlet, *Rock'n'Roll Mamma*, was published by Flarestack and her first full collection, *The Kitchen of Lovely Contraptions* (flipped eye) was developed with funding from Arts Council England and nominated for The Aldeburgh First Collection Prize.

Lawrence Schimel was born in New York and has lived in Madrid, Spain for nearly 15 years. He is the author of two poetry collections in English, *Fairy Tales for Writers* and *Deleted Names*, and one in Spanish, *Desayuno en la cama*, as well as a collection of erotic short stories, *His Tongue*.

Stephen Sexton lives in Belfast where he's working towards a PhD at the Seamus Heaney Centre for Poetry. He was the winner of the inaugural Funeral Services Northern Ireland National Poetry Competition. His poems have appeared in *The Open Ear*, *Abridged*, and as part of the Lifeboat series of readings.

Jon Stone was born in Derby and is currently London-based. His collection, *School of Forgery*, was a Poetry Book Society recommendation and he won an Eric Gregory Award in 2012. He's also co-creator of Sidekick Books (www.drfulminare.com), publishers of collaborative creative anthologies.

Sara-Mae Tuson has had short fiction, poetry and articles published in the Salt anthology *Overheard*, *The Journal*, *Ink, Sweat and Tears*, *Inky Needles*, *Rising*, *Obsessed with Pipework*, *The London Magazine* and more. She has performed as a guest at Loose Muse, Angel Poetry, The Hot House and Book Club Boutique.

Ruth Wiggins lives in East London with her partner and three sons. Her poetry has appeared in *Brittle Star*, *Smiths Knoll* and several anthologies. When not writing poetry, she enjoys hiking and photography; her book of women dressed as super heroes was published in 2008: amostoys.com/wwoa. She is a member of Forest Poets.

Jerrold Yam is a law undergraduate at University College London and the author of *Scattered Vertebrae* (2013) and *Chasing Curtained Suns* (2012). His poems have been published in over sixty literary journals and anthologies worldwide. He has been awarded poetry prizes from Arts Council England, the British Council and the National University of Singapore, and is the youngest Singaporean to be nominated for the Pushcart Prize.

About the editors

Rachel Piercey studied English Literature at St Hugh's College, Oxford, where she won the Newdigate Prize in 2008 with her poem *Returning, 1945*. Her pamphlet of illustrated love poems, *The Flower and the Plough*, was published by The Emma Press in January 2013.

Emma Wright studied Classics at Brasenose College, Oxford. She worked in ebook production at Orion Publishing Group before leaving to set up The Emma Press in 2012. She lives in Winnersh.

THE EMMA PRESS

The Emma Press is an independent publisher which was founded by Emma Wright in 2012. It publishes mostly poetry and is dedicated to producing books which are sweet, funny and easy on the eye. The Emma Press Picks, a series of themed single-author pamphlets, will be released from 2014 onwards.

Sign up to the Emma Press newsletter and hear about upcoming events and publications, as well as opportunities to submit to future projects.

http://theemmapress.com

ALSO FROM THE EMMA PRESS

the flower and the plough

a beautiful book of love poems by Rachel Piercey,
illustrated by Emma Wright

Piercey's oscillations between lover's ecstasy and love poet's objectivity are so deft that her analytical lens becomes as much a fascination as the amorous perspective on which it focuses.
— Andrew Wynn Owen, *The Oxonian Review*

On sale at theemmapress.com

COMING SOON FROM THE EMMA PRESS

a poetic primer to love and seduction:

naso was my tutor

An instructional guide to sex and relationships, inspired by the Roman poet Ovid's *Ars Amatoria* and *Remedia Amoris*. This anthology is a mixture of satire on modern romantic tropes and some genuinely helpful advice from contemporary poets.

If you've got the voice for it, sing; if your limbs are supple, dance; and whatever else you can do to please, do that too.
— Ovid, *Ars Amatoria*, Book I

Publishing January 2014

COMING SOON FROM THE EMMA PRESS

poems about homesickness and exile

An anthology themed around homesickness and exile, taking the Roman poet Ovid's *Tristia* as inspiration and broadening it to encompass meditations on identity, belonging, immigration, holidays, and the meaning of 'home'.

Publishing September 2014
Visit the website for more details.

http://theemmapress.com